To Yusra and Sara, and to anyone forced to become a refugee.
— R. F.

To my husband, Nizar. Thank you for believing in me every step of the way.
And to Sara and Mariam, my flowers. I'm always so proud of you!
— A. E.

Text copyright © 2023 Reem Faruqi
Illustrations copyright © 2023 Asma Enayeh

First published in 2023 by Page Street Kids
an imprint of
Page Street Publishing Co.
27 Congress Street, Suite 1511
Salem, MA 01970
www.pagestreetpublishing.com

Distributed by Macmillan, sales in Canada by The Canadian Manda Group

23 24 25 26 27 CCO 5 4 3 2 1

ISBN-13: 978-1-64567-983-7
ISBN-10: 1-64567-983-7

CIP data for this book is available from the Library of Congress.

This book was typeset in Korinth Serial, Avallon All Caps, and Little Jack.
The illustrations were done with watercolor and gouache.
Book design by Julia Tyler and Melia Parsloe for Page Street Kids
Cover design by Katie Beasley for Page Street Kids
Edited by Kayla Tostevin for Page Street Kids

Printed and bound in Shenzhen, Guangdong, China

Page Street Publishing uses only materials from suppliers who are committed to
responsible and sustainable forest management.

Page Street Publishing protects our planet by donating to nonprofits like The Trustees,
which focuses on local land conservation.

Bibliography available at the QR code below, or this link:
https://www.pagestreetpublishing.com/swimming-toward-a-dream

Swimming Toward a Dream
Page Street Kids

SWIMMING TOWARD A DREAM

Yusra Mardini's Incredible Journey from Refugee to Olympic Swimmer

written by Reem Faruqi   illustrated by Asma Enayeh

PAGE STREET KIDS

In a sandy suburb dotted with jasmine flowers of Damascus, Syria,
Yusra sees a pool for the first time and cries.

She flounders because she cannot
touch the bottom.

Water burns her nose.

Finally, when she stops fighting and trusts
the water, she floats in peace.

Slowly, she learns to bob up
and down.

One breath at a time.

Before she can walk,
Yusra Mardini learns to swim.

With time and her father's coaching,
she dives deeper, swims swifter, and dreams bigger.

At fourteen years old, she represents Syria in the International Swimming Federation World Championships and races in competitions all over the world, winning medal after medal.

She leaves a trail of swimmers and bubbles behind her. Bubbles of faith. Faith that if she trains hard enough, she will make it to the Olympics.

One breath at a time.

Every day after school, Yusra rushes to swim practice.
Underwater, in her blue cocoon, Yusra's worries float away.

But on land, the world is changing. Yusra and the people of Damascus, Syria, are afraid to go outside. War crashes down.

Now, when Yusra swims the backstroke, the sky winces down at her through a broken roof.

Yusra's school is canceled for days at a time.
Her swim training is canceled, too. Peeking outside her
home, Yusra wonders . . .

Is it safe to swim today?
Will more friends move away? When will peace return?

She tries to relax,

one breath at a time.

But Yusra's dreams of diving into Olympic waters drown when bombs whistle down on her swimming pool.

Two of her father's cousins are fleeing to Germany. They can take Yusra and her big sister, Sara, with them. Hope pours into Yusra's heart as she dreams of a better future and the chance to swim again.

Tears clog her throat when she hugs her mother and little sister goodbye.

As countries close their doors, Yusra and Sara are forced to fly
to Turkey, then sneak into Europe on foot or by sea.

The boat from Turkey to Greece is for six people.
Twenty are crammed onto it. Some passengers cry. All pray.

The Aegean Sea is nothing like Yusra's blue swimming pool cocoon.

This water is endless.

The boat groans and tilts.
Suddenly, the loud motor becomes silent.

Water rushes in.
Panic floods Yusra's chest.

Turning back is not an option.

To make the boat lighter, a few passengers take turns in the swirling sea.

Yusra gasps in the cold water. Hard breaths of fear. Yusra and Sara are the only strong swimmers, but strong enough to swim the rest of the way?

The boat's rope cuts Yusra's hands.
She sees land, but angry waves spin the boat farther away.

The sisters steer the boat toward the Greek shore,

one breath at a time.

They kick.

They push.

They pull.

But without the motor, it's not enough.

They are at the mercy of the sea for three and a half hours.
Two hundred and ten minutes. Twelve thousand and six hundred seconds.

Yusra looks up at the faces on the boat. A little boy smiles down at her.
Even though her body is numb, she makes funny faces up at him.

Yusra holds on,

one breath at a time.

Finally, a roar.

Soon, Sara feels the rocky bottom.
Land!

Although they are out of the perilous waters, danger still flows around them. Yusra and Sara keep traveling. Greece to Macedonia to Serbia to Hungary to Austria.

Their feet ache because taxis do not stop for them.

Their stomachs grumble because they are not served in restaurants in Greece.

Their hearts sink when they are turned away from the trains in Hungary.

After twenty-five long and frightening days, the sisters reach their refugee camp in Berlin, Germany.

Once she has food to eat and a safe place to sleep, Yusra's Olympic dreams float back into her mind. But, having missed months of training, Yusra no longer leaves a trail of swimmers behind her.

She wakes at the white thread of dawn to practice at a nearby swimming club.

One breath at a time,

Yusra gets faster. She believes she can make it to the 2020 Tokyo Olympics.

Yusra's dream comes true sooner than she expected. She gasps and squeals when she gets an important email: the International Olympics Committee has asked her to swim in the 2016 Olympics on the first-ever Refugee Team.

Months after leaving Syria behind, Yusra Mardini stands on the starting block in Rio de Janeiro, Brazil.

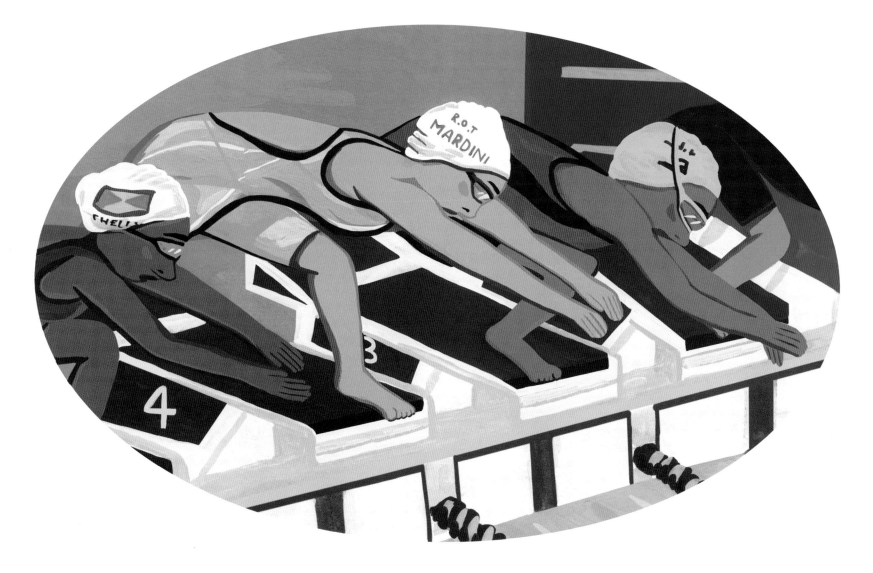

As she dives back into her blue cocoon,
her Olympic dreams float at last.

Now, Yusra stands as an ambassador for the United Nations Refugee Agency and an Olympic flag bearer, walking in pride.

Refugee Olympic Team

She wants to make sure the voices of refugees are heard.
She knows she can change the world.

One breath at a time.

1 DARAYYA, SYRIA

1998 — **March 5:** Yusra is born in the Darayya suburb of Damascus, Syria.

2010 — **Fall:** At 12 years old, Yusra makes it onto the Syrian National team.

2011 — **March 15:** The Syrian Civil War begins when Yusra is 13 years old.

2012 — **August 20-25:** The Darayya Massacre takes place. Yusra's home is destroyed.

December 15: At 14 years old, Yusra competes for Syria in the International Swimming Federation Championships.

2015 — **August 12:** At 17 years old, Yusra leaves Syria with her big sister, Sara; their father's two cousins; and other refugees.

2 BEIRUT, LEBANON

Yusra and Sara reach Beirut by plane.

3 IZMIR, TURKEY

Yusra and Sara reach Izmir by plane. Here, they take a boat with eighteen other refugees to Greece. On their first attempt on the boat, they are caught by border agents and sent back. On their next attempt, the engine dies after about twenty minutes, and the dinghy takes on water. Passengers throw their bags overboard. The sisters and a few male passengers take turns in the choppy Aegean Sea to keep the boat afloat. Finally, the engine turns back on. However, since the boat is too slow, Sara jumps back in to help lighten the boat so it can reach land sooner.

4 LESBOS, GREECE

After three and a half hours in the sea, the passengers reach Lesbos. Yusra witnesses

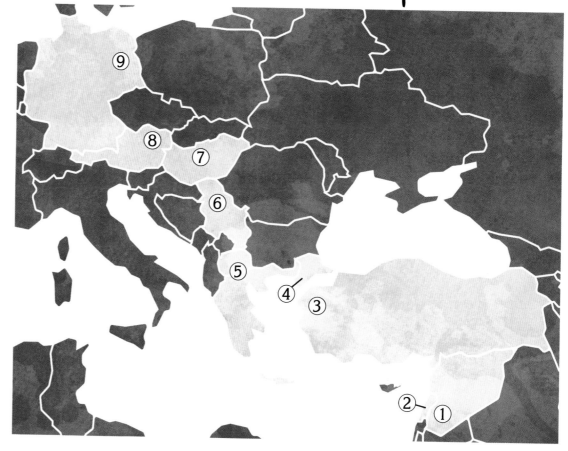

Yusra's Journey

kindness when a girl gives her shoes. But in many parts of Europe, refugees are not welcome. Yusra deals with struggles such as taxis not stopping for them, restaurants turning them away, and being banned from riding the trains. From Greece, they travel by land, walking and taking trains and buses to…

5 MACEDONIA-GREECE BORDER

6 BELGRADE, SERBIA

7 BUDAPEST, HUNGARY

8 VIENNA, AUSTRIA

9 BERLIN, GERMANY

September: 25 days after leaving Syria, Yusra and Sara reach Berlin.

December 23: Yusra's parents and little sister reach Berlin after fleeing Syria. The family lives together in Germany.

Author's Note

When Yusra qualified for The Refugee Olympic Team and competed in the Rio 2016 Olympics, she said, "I want to represent all the refugees because I want to show everyone that after the pain and after the storm comes calm days." Yusra placed first in her heat, but it wasn't enough to qualify for the semi-finals. She is remembered for saving the lives of her boat passengers and for making it to the Olympics during the Refugee Crisis. Someday she would like to become a pilot, but right now her focus remains in the water. She is still swimming and qualified for, competed, and was a flag-bearer in the 2021 Tokyo Olympics.

Yusra also serves as an avid advocate for refugees. In April 2017, the UNHCR, the UN Refugee Agency, appointed Yusra Mardini as the youngest ever Goodwill Ambassador. Yusra wants to convey the message that refugees can dream and be successful just like anyone else. Currently, she has three dreams: "I hope that they will open the borders for refugees, and I hope to get a medal in the Olympics, and that my home town is in peace again."

I hope Yusra's journey inspires you to welcome refugees, never give up, and to always follow your dreams.

Illustrator's Note

As a woman growing up in Damascus, the jasmine-scented city of nerium and bougainvillea, it was painful to witness its destruction and that of the rest of beloved Syria. Illustrating the heroic story of Yusra Mardini and her sister Sara with all my feelings is a dedication to all the refugees who had to cross the horrific seas to escape the carnage in Syria. I hope illustrating this beautiful story of courage and perseverance can bring light and hope for the little ones.